I0150474

40 Days of
Greater Peace

Coloring Prayer Companion

ALEXANDRA KUBEBATU

All Scripture derives from the New American Bible, Revised Edition (NABRE)

40 Days of Greater Peace Coloring Prayer Companion

Copyright © 2016 Alexandra Kubebatu

Cover Design and Illustrations by Alexandra Kubebatu

ISBN: 978-0692703588

40DaysOfGreater.com
Prayer Journals & Coloring Prayer Companions

Ask about special pricing for fundraisers, parishes, ministries, and apostolates via email: Support@40DaysOfGreater.com

THIS COLORING PRAYER COMPANION BELONGS TO:

_____

40 Days of
Greater Peace

Coloring Prayer Companion

Your will, Lord be done in me in every way and manner that You, my Lord, want. If You want it to be done with trials, strengthen me and let them come; if with persecutions, illnesses, dishonors, and a lack of life's necessities, here I am; I will not turn away, my Father, nor is it right that I turn my back on You.

-Saint Teresa of Avila, excerpt from *The Way of Perfection*

May the peace of Christ be with you
now and forever.

40DaysOfGreater.com
Prayer Journals & Coloring Prayer Companions

My Visual Prayer

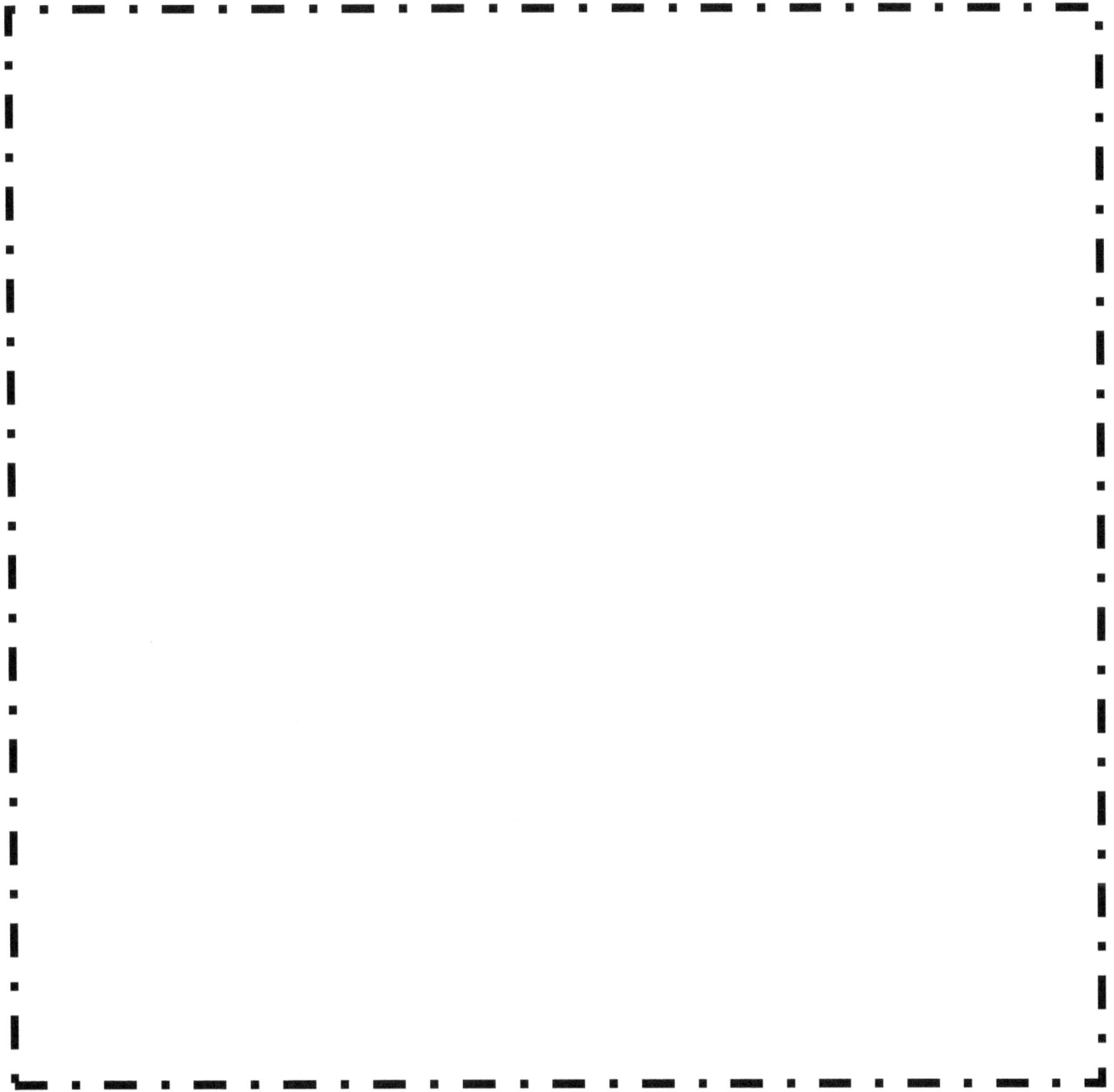

40DaysOfGreater.com
Prayer Journals & Coloring Prayer Companions

Do not be afraid of worldly matters
for they will pass away.

40DaysOfGreater.com
Prayer Journals & Coloring Prayer Companions

My Visual Prayer

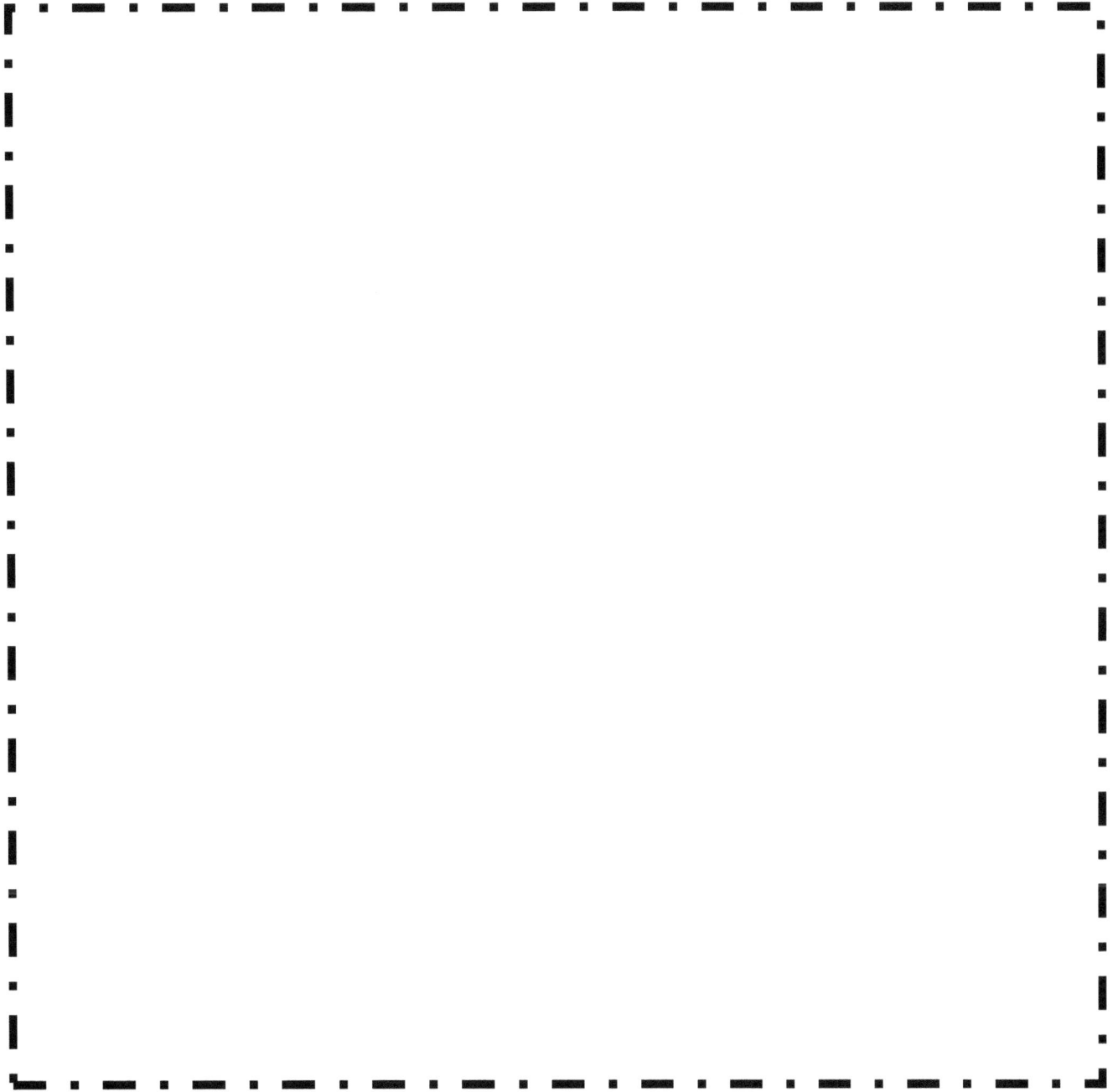

_____

_____

_____

_____

_____

40DaysOfGreater.com
Prayer Journals & Coloring Prayer Companions

Trust in the Lord.
He will never fail you.

40DaysOfGreater.com
Prayer Journals & Coloring Prayer Companions

My Visual Prayer

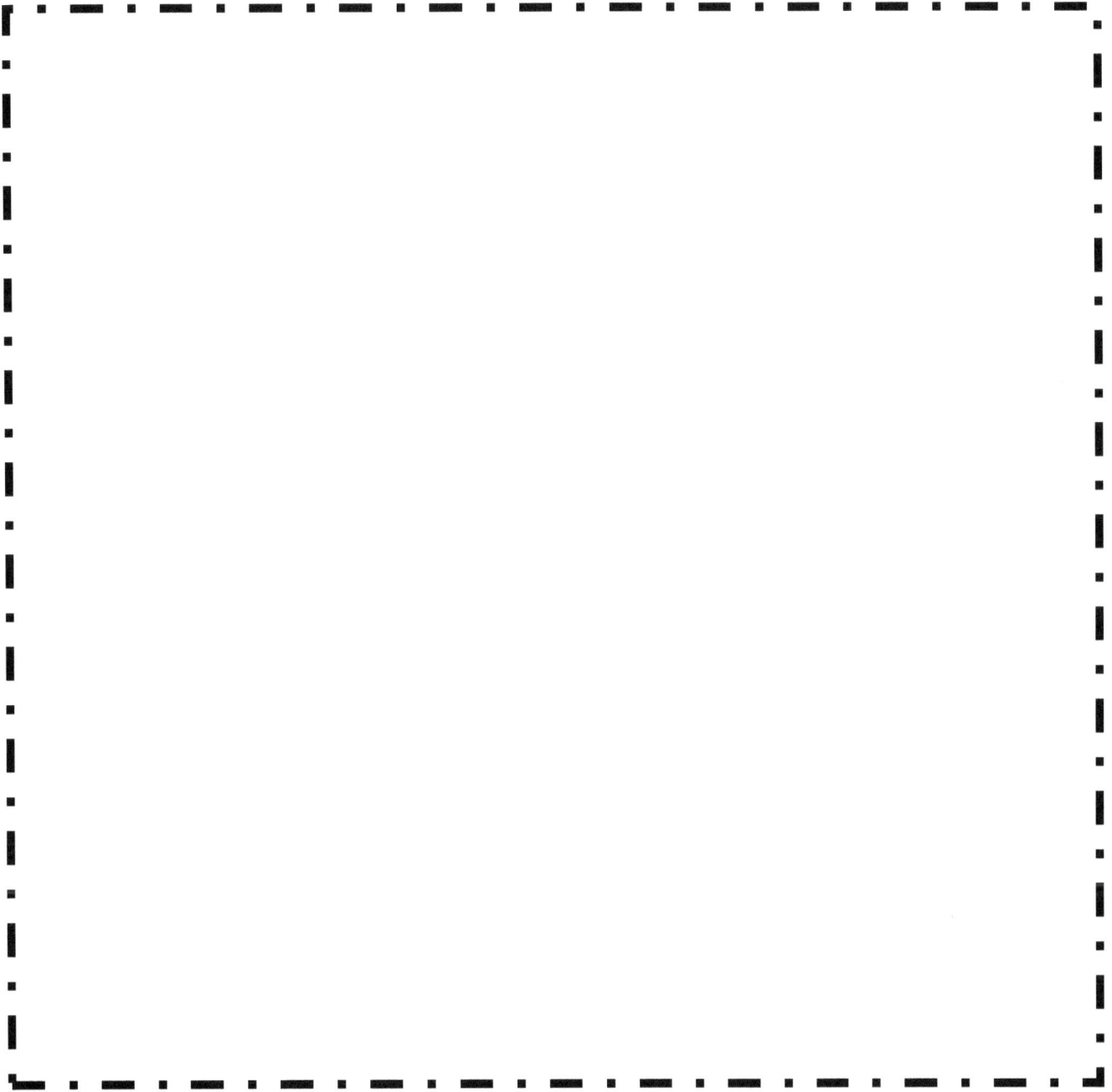

_____

_____

_____

_____

_____

40 Days of Greater Peace

40DaysOfGreater.com
Prayer Journals & Coloring Prayer Companions

Let go of anxieties and
let God heal your soul.

40DaysOfGreater.com
Prayer Journals & Coloring Prayer Companions

My Visual Prayer

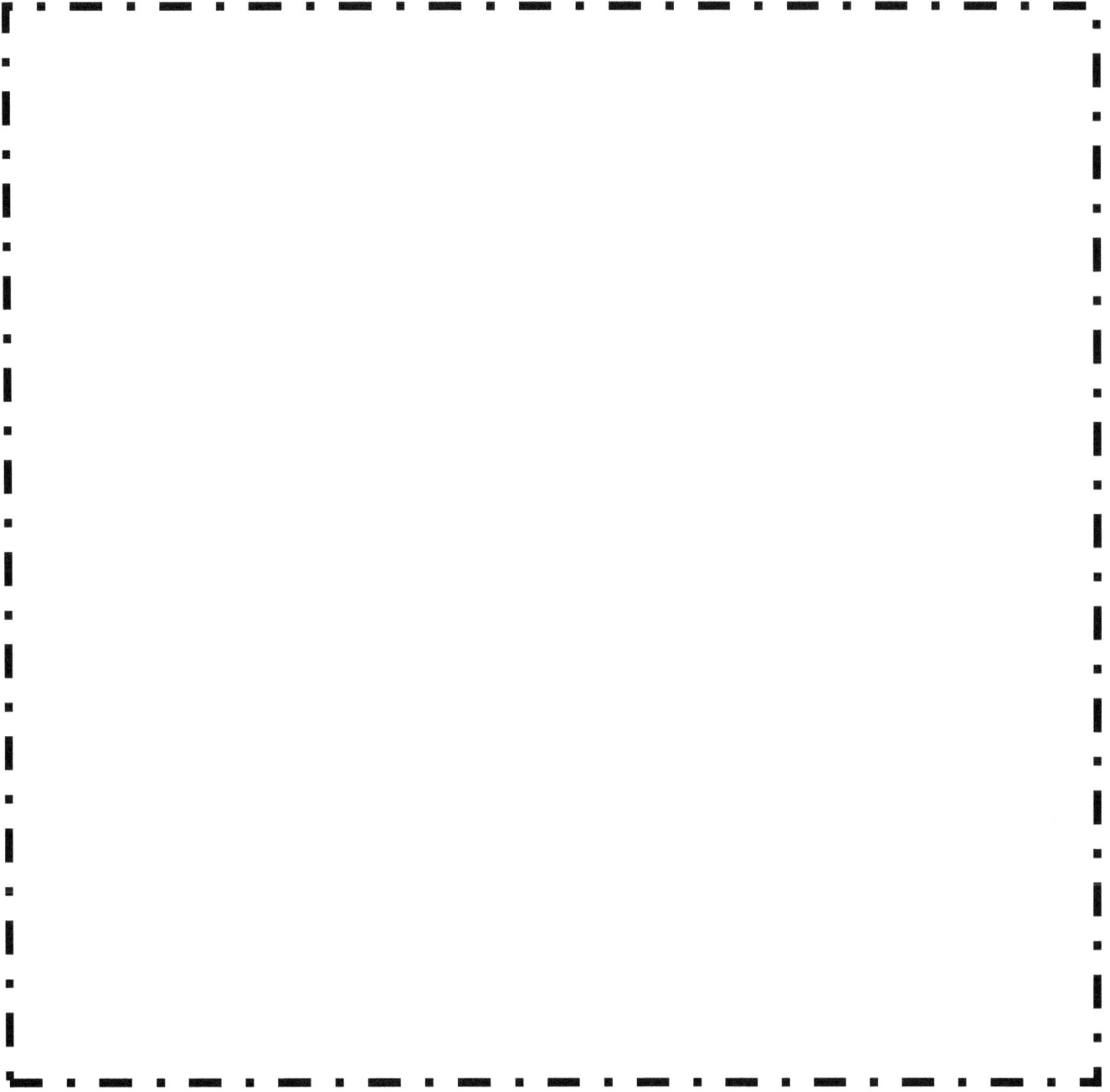

_____

_____

_____

_____

_____

40DaysOfGreater.com
Prayer Journals & Coloring Prayer Companions

Rejoice for Jesus is with you!

40DaysOfGreater.com
Prayer Journals & Coloring Prayer Companions

My Visual Prayer

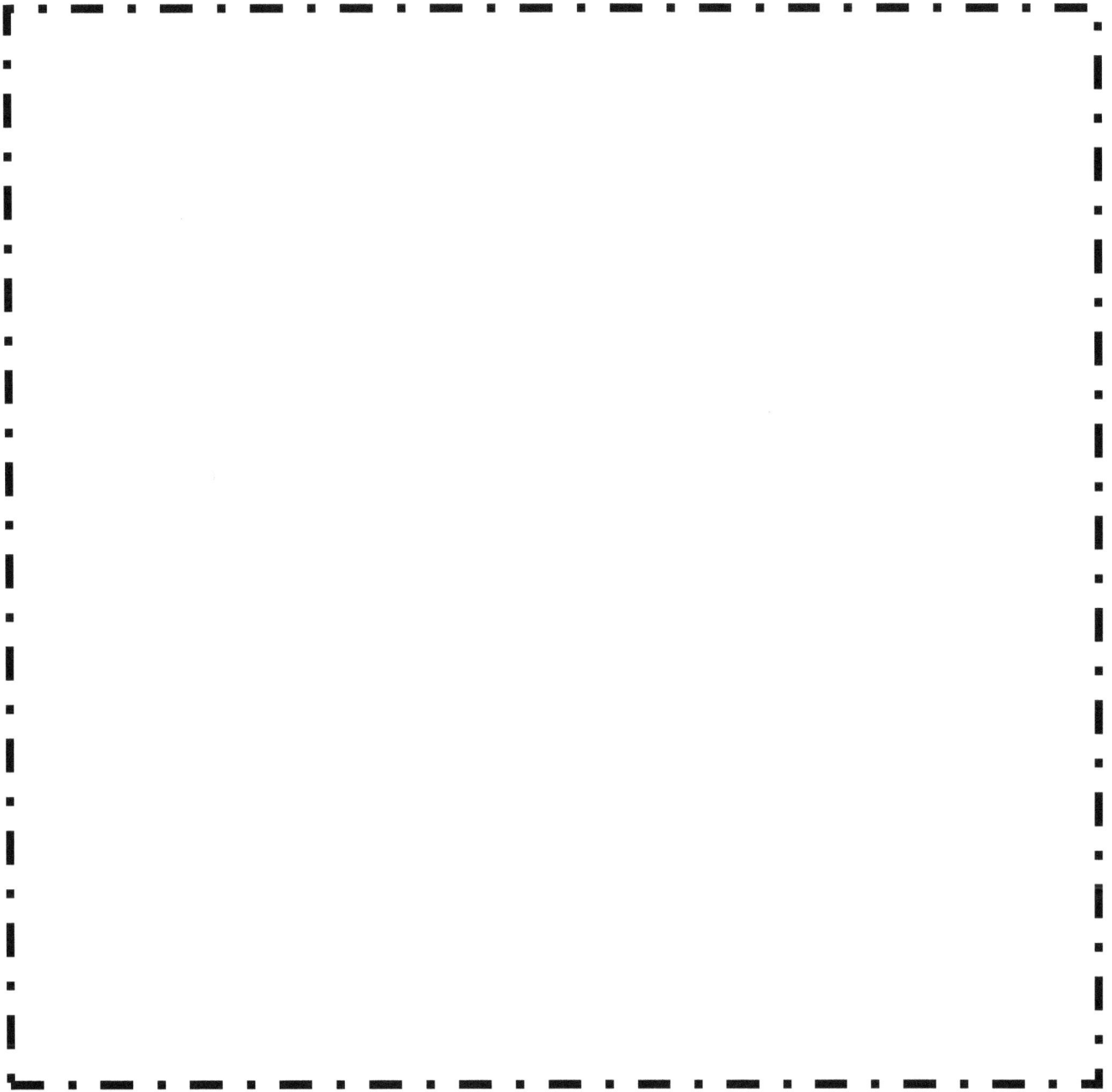

40DaysOfGreater.com
Prayer Journals & Coloring Prayer Companions

Feel the moment and
have the Lord's peace in the present.

40DaysOfGreater.com
Prayer Journals & Coloring Prayer Companions

My Visual Prayer

40DaysOfGreater.com
Prayer Journals & Coloring Prayer Companions

Do not worry. You are a child of God
and He created Heaven for you.

My Visual Prayer

All you need for your sanctification
is already before you.

40DaysOfGreater.com
Prayer Journals & Coloring Prayer Companions

My Visual Prayer

_____
_____
_____
_____
_____

40DaysOfGreater.com
Prayer Journals & Coloring Prayer Companions

The Lord of Peace heals
the anxious heart.

My Visual Prayer

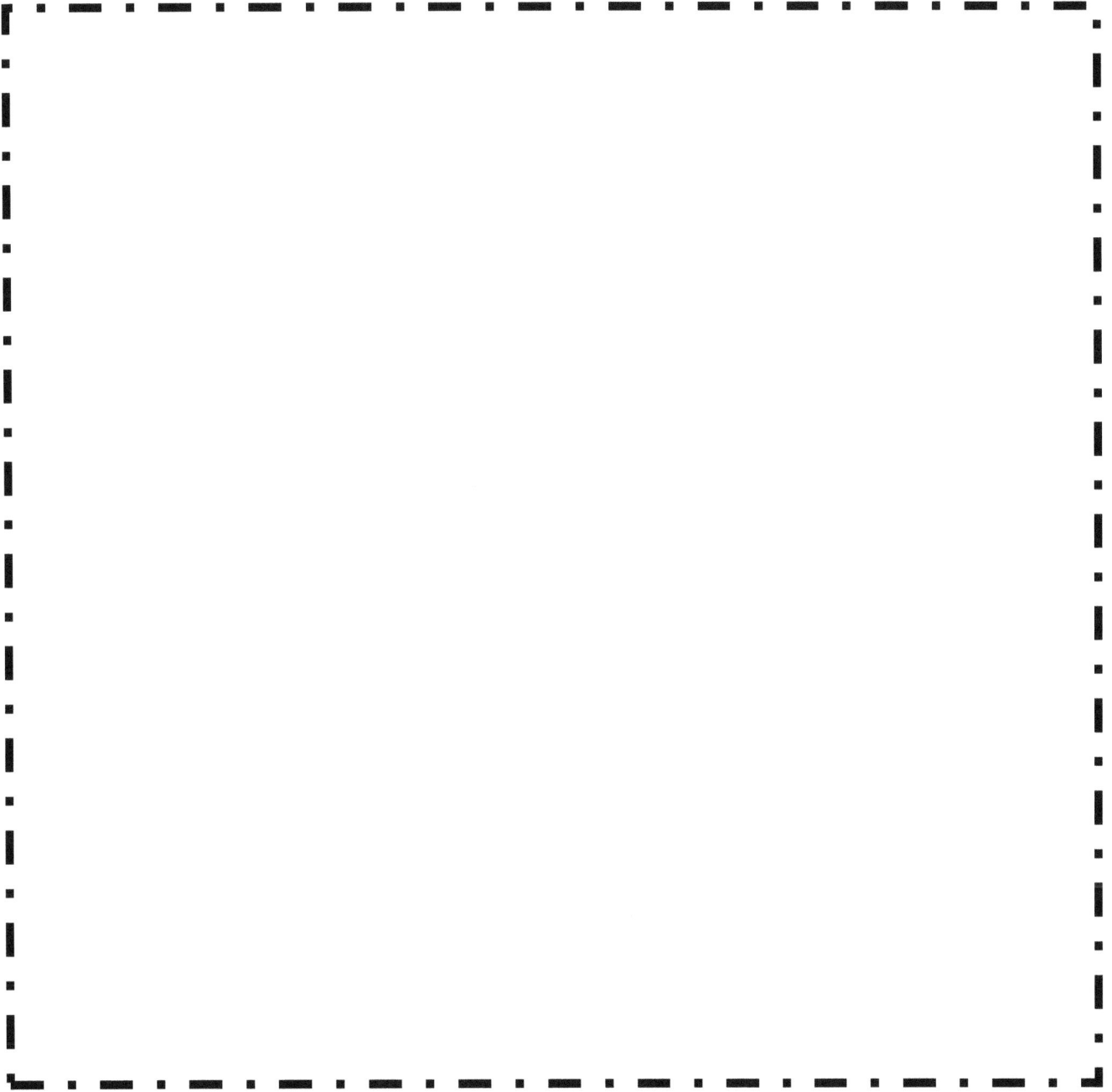

40DaysOfGreater.com
Prayer Journals & Coloring Prayer Companions

Allow the Holy Spirit to
rest within you.

40DaysOfGreater.com
Prayer Journals & Coloring Prayer Companions

My Visual Prayer

_____

_____

_____

_____

_____

40DaysOfGreater.com
Prayer Journals & Coloring Prayer Companions

Immerse the anxious mind in all things
of God and you will find peace.

40DaysOfGreater.com
Prayer Journals & Coloring Prayer Companions

My Visual Prayer

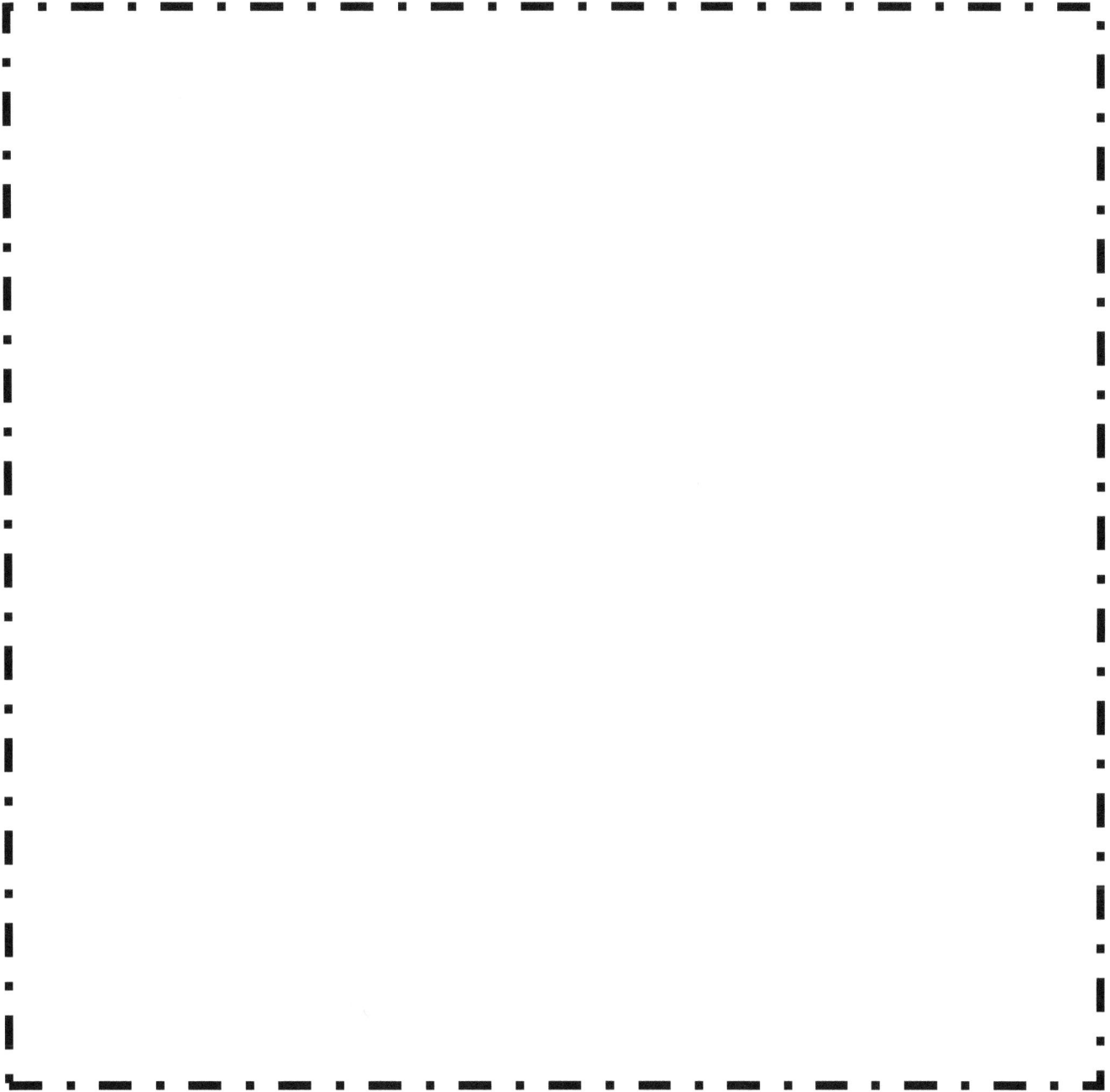

40DaysOfGreater.com
Prayer Journals & Coloring Prayer Companions

Take a deep breath and hold it. Exhale all your worries. Now breathe deeply and allow the love of God to fill your soul.

My Visual Prayer

_____
_____
_____
_____
_____

God has never abandoned you.

40DaysOfGreater.com
Prayer Journals & Coloring Prayer Companions

My Visual Prayer

Worry drains the joy that comes from a faithful heart.

40DaysOfGreater.com
Prayer Journals & Coloring Prayer Companions

My Visual Prayer

Peace is a fruit of the Holy Spirit
working through you.

My Visual Prayer

_____
_____
_____
_____
_____

May Jesus Christ grant you His peace
through the Holy Spirit.

My Visual Prayer

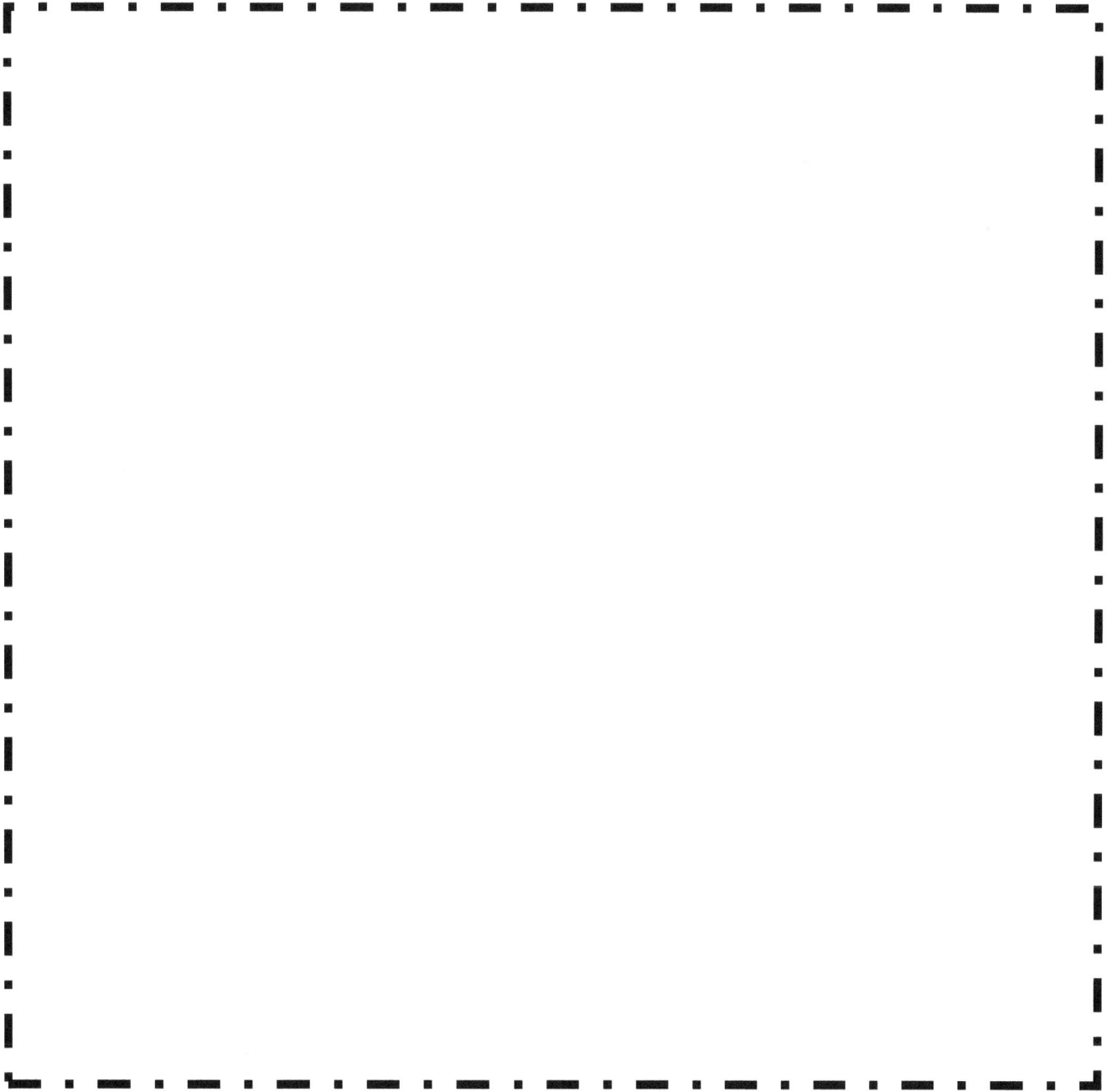

40DaysOfGreater.com
Prayer Journals & Coloring Prayer Companions

Why do you fear the future? It does not exist. The present is the only reality.

40DaysOfGreater.com
Prayer Journals & Coloring Prayer Companions

My Visual Prayer

_____
_____
_____
_____
_____

Do not let the worries and fears of others affect you. Choose to stay at peace and pray for them.

40DaysOfGreater.com
Prayer Journals & Coloring Prayer Companions

My Visual Prayer

_____

_____

_____

_____

_____

40 Days of Greater Peace

40DaysOfGreater.com
Prayer Journals & Coloring Prayer Companions

Walk hand-in-hand with Jesus
and allow Him to carry you
when necessary.

40DaysOfGreater.com
Prayer Journals & Coloring Prayer Companions

My Visual Prayer

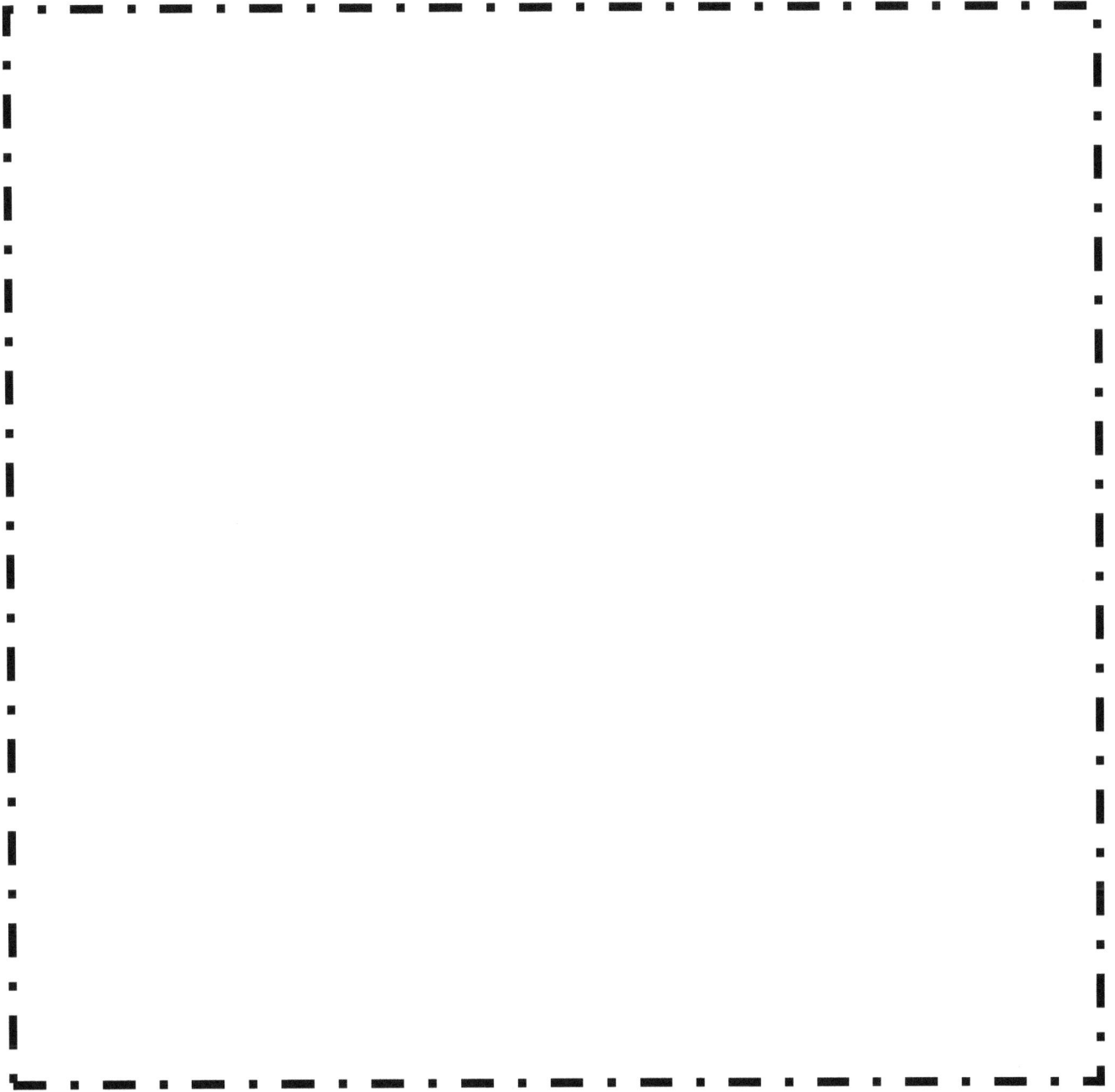

_____

_____

_____

_____

_____

Place your hardships in God's hands,
not your own.

40DaysOfGreater.com
Prayer Journals & Coloring Prayer Companions

My Visual Prayer

May the peace of Christ be with you
now and forever.

My Visual Prayer

40DaysOfGreater.com
Prayer Journals & Coloring Prayer Companions

Do not be afraid of worldly matters for
they will pass away.

40DaysOfGreater.com
Prayer Journals & Coloring Prayer Companions

My Visual Prayer

_____

_____

_____

_____

_____

Trust in the Lord.
He will never fail you.

40DaysOfGreater.com
Prayer Journals & Coloring Prayer Companions

My Visual Prayer

Let go of anxieties and
let God heal your soul.

40DaysOfGreater.com
Prayer Journals & Coloring Prayer Companions

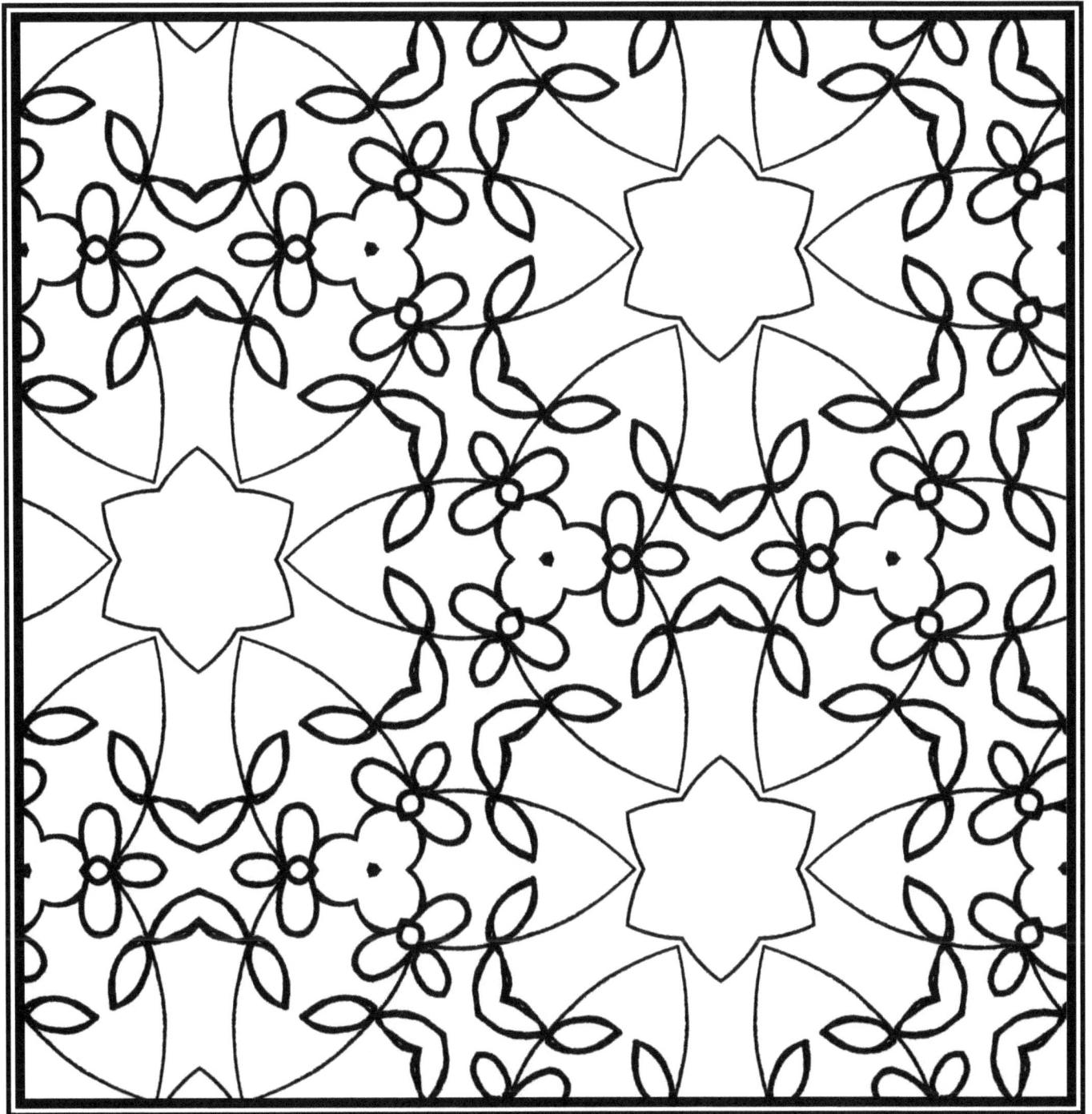

Rejoice for Jesus is with you!

My Visual Prayer

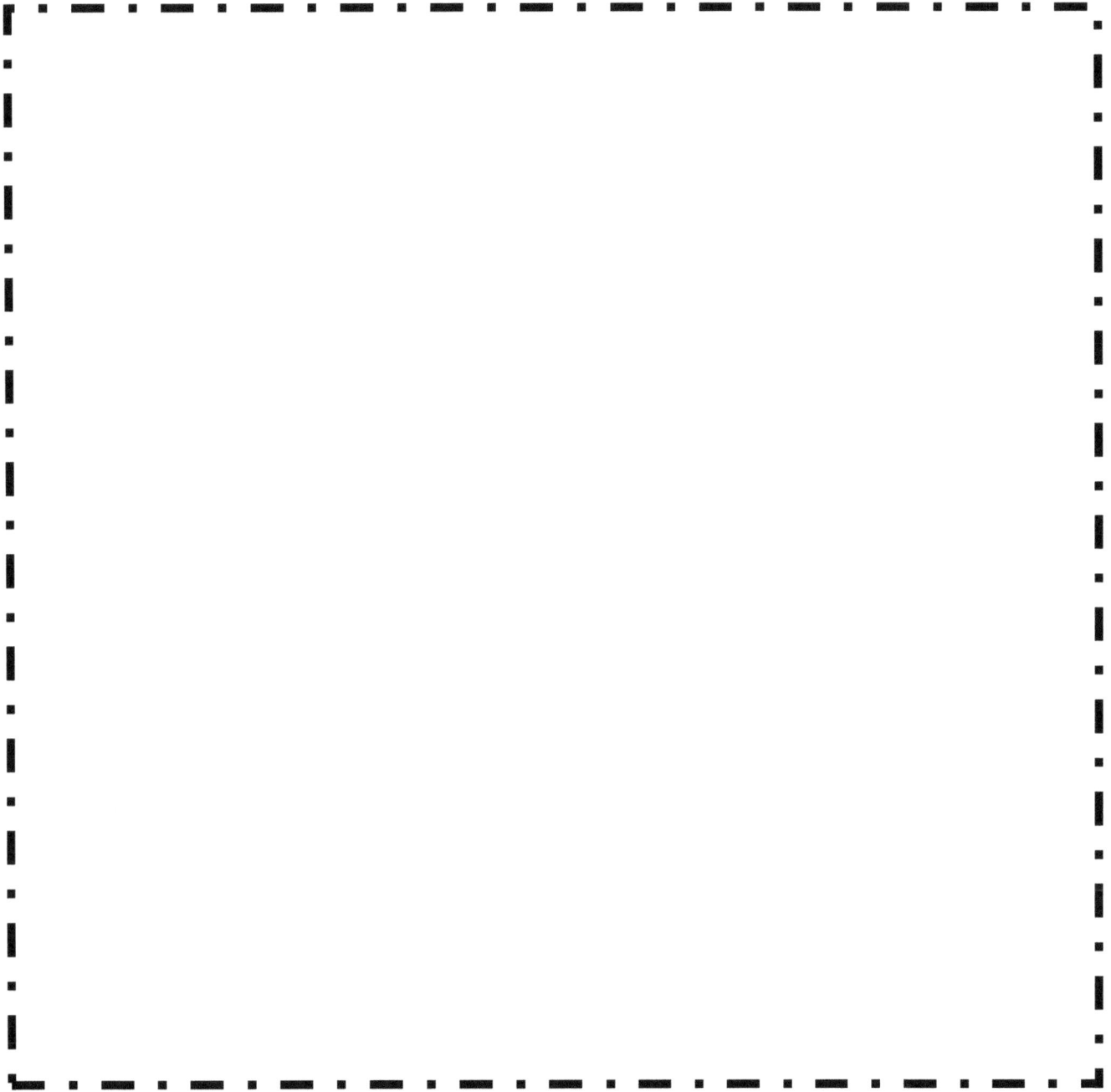

40DaysOfGreater.com
Prayer Journals & Coloring Prayer Companions

Feel the moment and have the Lord's
peace in the present.

40DaysOfGreater.com
Prayer Journals & Coloring Prayer Companions

My Visual Prayer

40DaysOfGreater.com
Prayer Journals & Coloring Prayer Companions

Do not worry. You are a child of God
and He created Heaven for you.

My Visual Prayer

All you need for your sanctification
is already before you.

40DaysOfGreater.com
Prayer Journals & Coloring Prayer Companions

My Visual Prayer

40DaysOfGreater.com
Prayer Journals & Coloring Prayer Companions

The Lord of Peace heals
the anxious heart.

My Visual Prayer

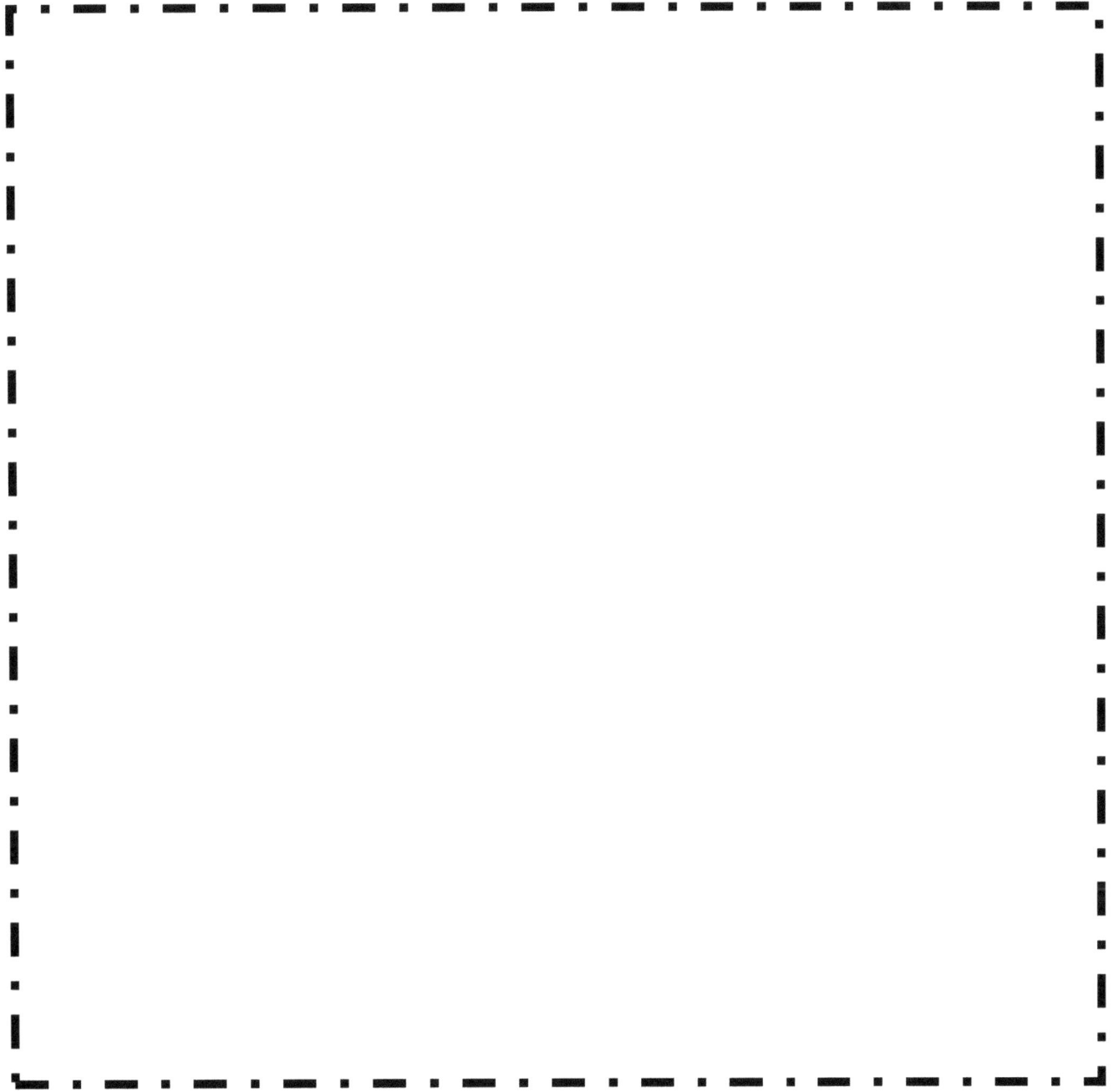

_____

_____

_____

_____

_____

40 Days of Greater Peace

40DaysOfGreater.com
Prayer Journals & Coloring Prayer Companions

Immerse the anxious mind in all things
of God and you will find peace.

40DaysOfGreater.com
Prayer Journals & Coloring Prayer Companions

My Visual Prayer

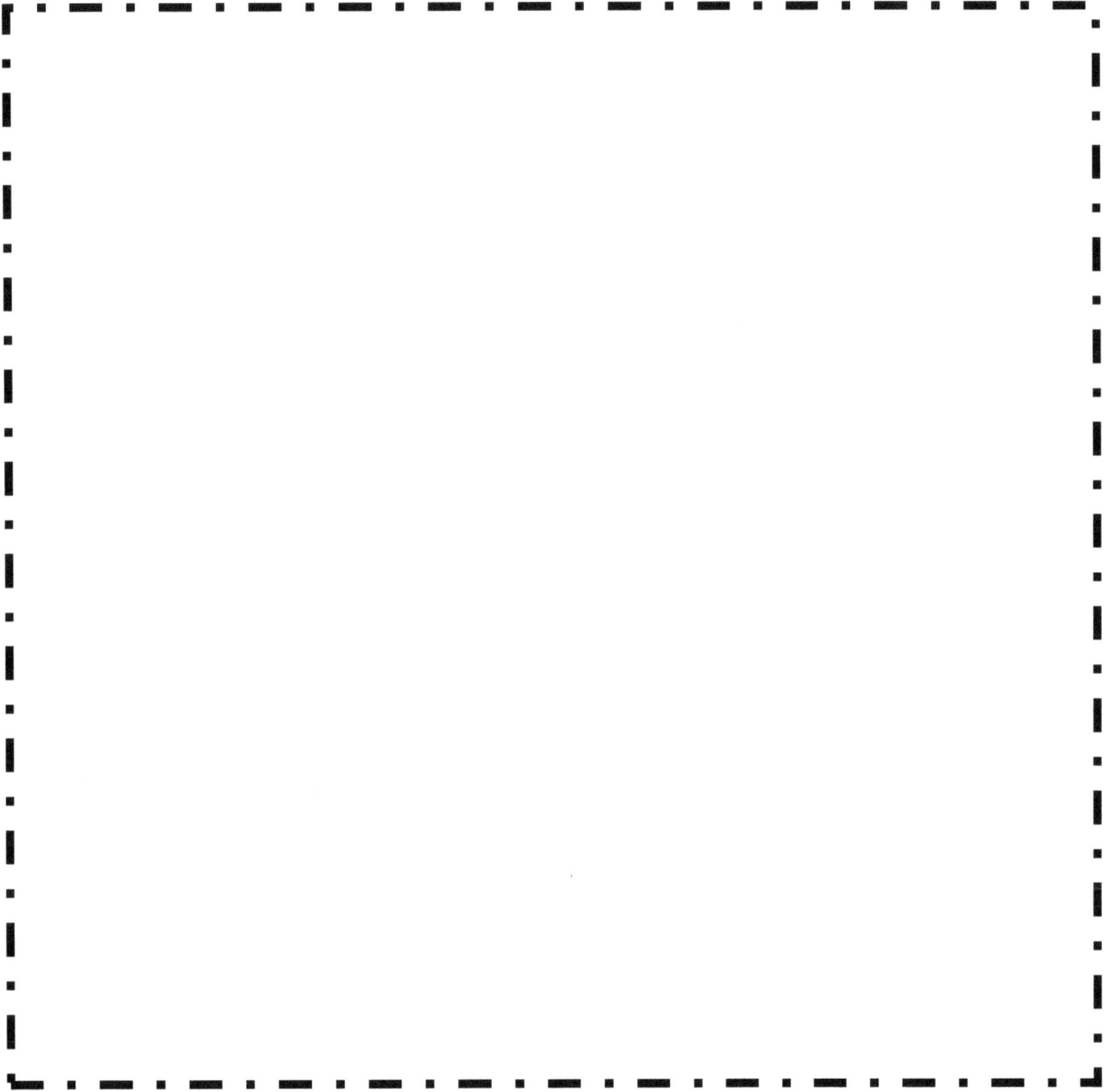

40DaysOfGreater.com
Prayer Journals & Coloring Prayer Companions

Take a deep breath and hold it. Exhale all
your worries. Now breathe deeply and
allow the love of God to fill your soul.

40DaysOfGreater.com
Prayer Journals & Coloring Prayer Companions

My Visual Prayer

40 Days of Greater Peace

40DaysOfGreater.com
Prayer Journals & Coloring Prayer Companions

God has never abandoned you.

40DaysOfGreater.com
Prayer Journals & Coloring Prayer Companions

My Visual Prayer

_____
_____
_____
_____
_____

40DaysOfGreater.com
Prayer Journals & Coloring Prayer Companions

Worry drains the joy that comes from a faithful heart.

40DaysOfGreater.com
Prayer Journals & Coloring Prayer Companions

My Visual Prayer

_____

_____

_____

_____

_____

Peace is a fruit of the Holy Spirit
working through you.

40DaysOfGreater.com
Prayer Journals & Coloring Prayer Companions

My Visual Prayer

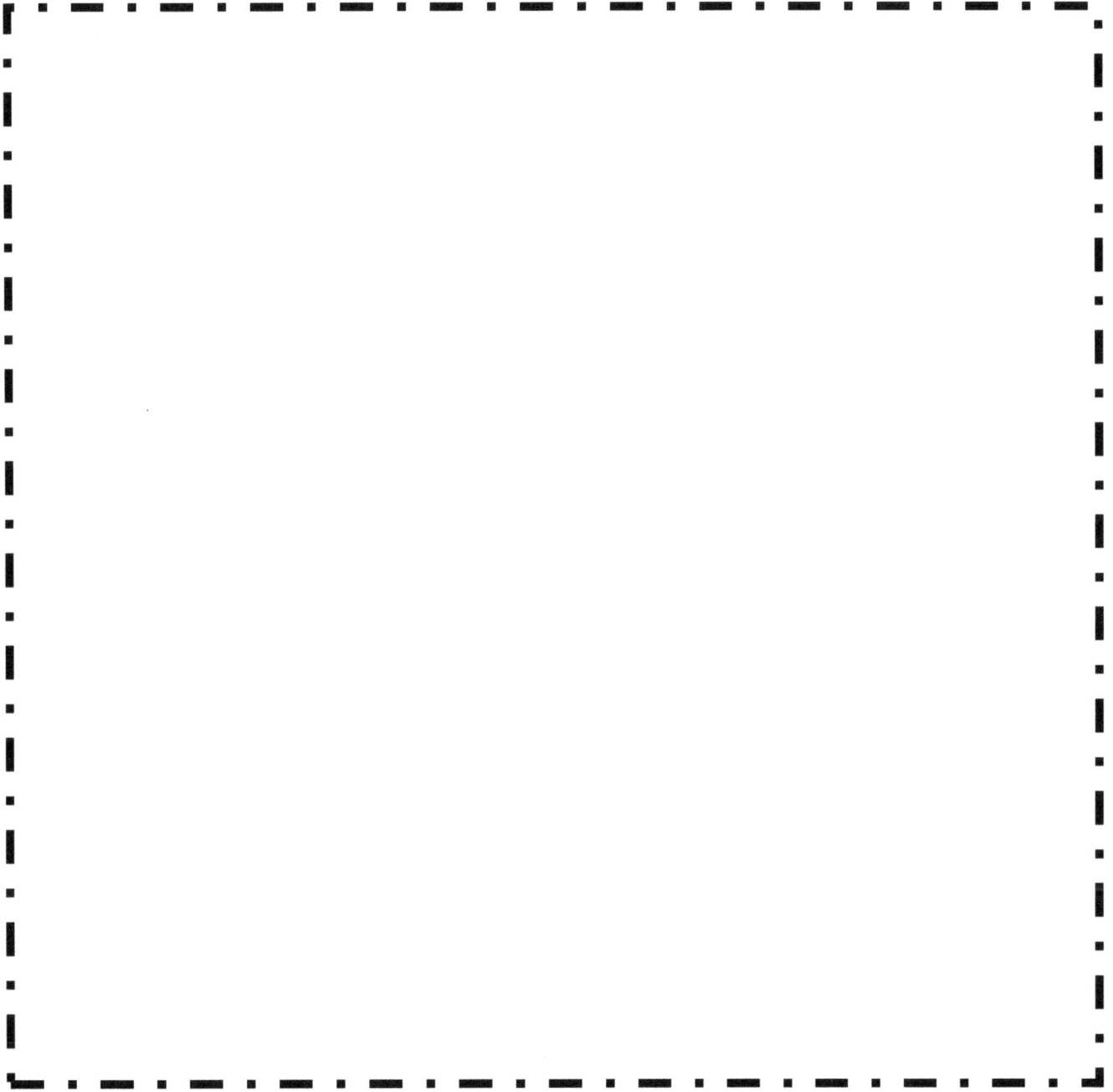

_____

_____

_____

_____

_____

40 Days of Greater Peace

40DaysOfGreater.com

Prayer Journals & Coloring Prayer Companions

May Jesus Christ grant you His peace
through the Holy Spirit.

40DaysOfGreater.com
Prayer Journals & Coloring Prayer Companions

My Visual Prayer

40DaysOfGreater.com
Prayer Journals & Coloring Prayer Companions

Why do you fear the future? It does not exist. The present is the only reality.

40DaysOfGreater.com
Prayer Journals & Coloring Prayer Companions

My Visual Prayer

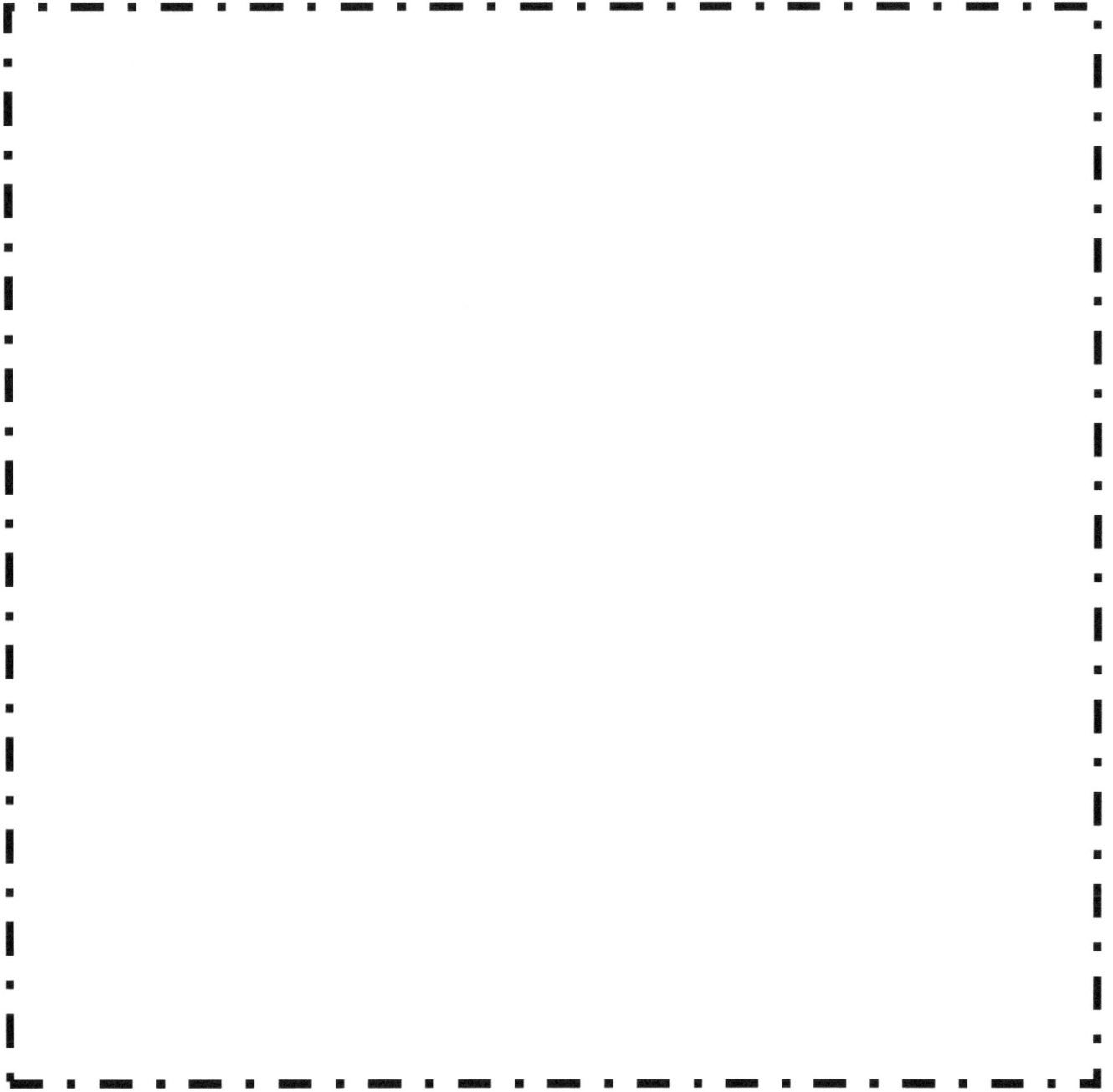

_____

_____

_____

_____

_____

40DaysOfGreater.com
Prayer Journals & Coloring Prayer Companions

Do not let the worries and fears of others
affect you. Choose to stay at peace
and pray for them.

40DaysOfGreater.com
Prayer Journals & Coloring Prayer Companions

My Visual Prayer

40DaysOfGreater.com
Prayer Journals & Coloring Prayer Companions

Walk hand-in-hand with Jesus and allow Him to carry you when necessary.

40DaysOfGreater.com
Prayer Journals & Coloring Prayer Companions

My Visual Prayer

Place your struggles in God's hands,
not your own.

40DaysOfGreater.com
Prayer Journals & Coloring Prayer Companions

My Visual Prayer

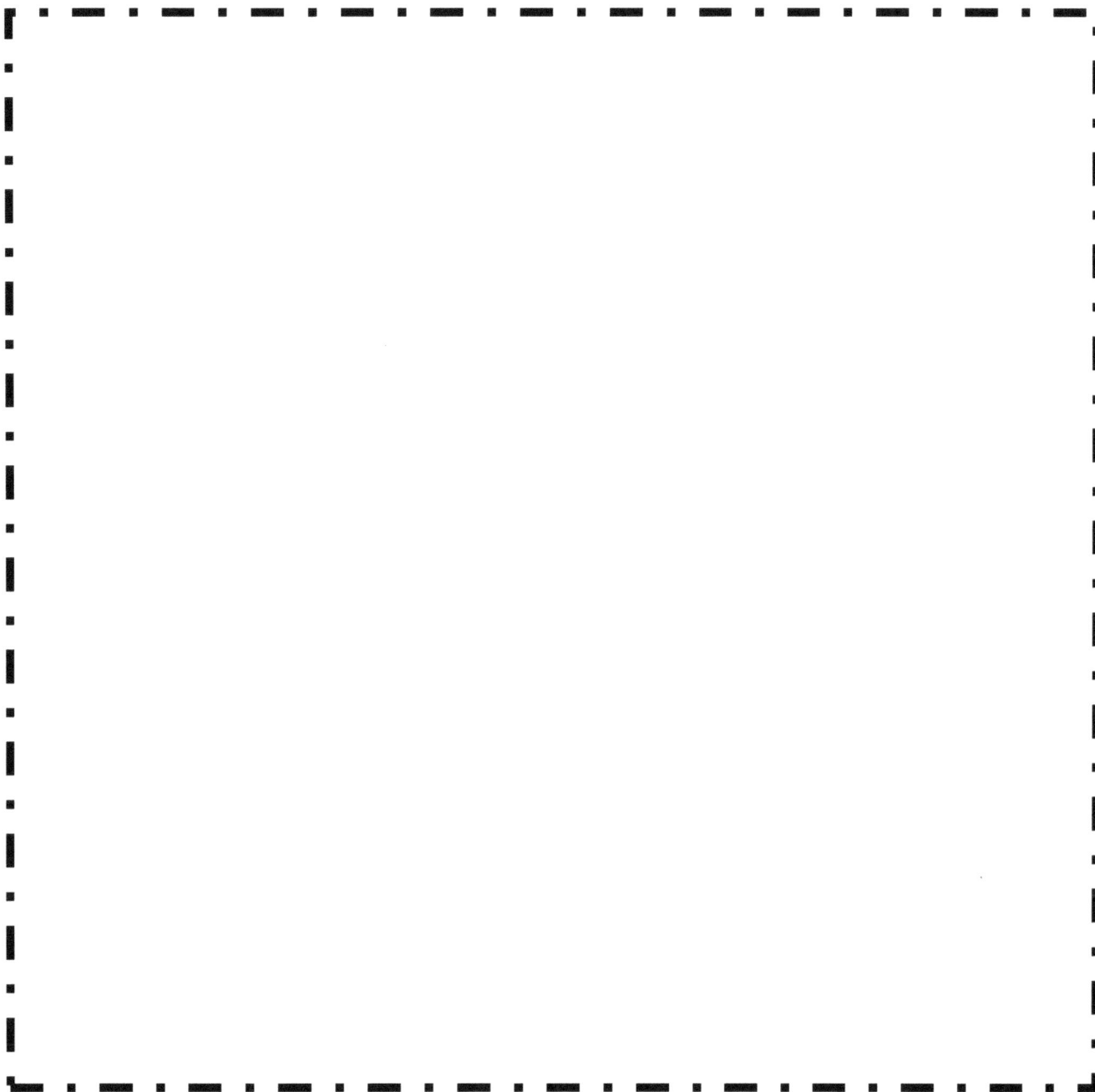

_____

_____

_____

_____

_____

40DaysOfGreater.com
Prayer Journals & Coloring Prayer Companions

Fear and worry place you in a spiritual desert away from God's love and peace.

40DaysOfGreater.com
Prayer Journals & Coloring Prayer Companions

My Visual Prayer

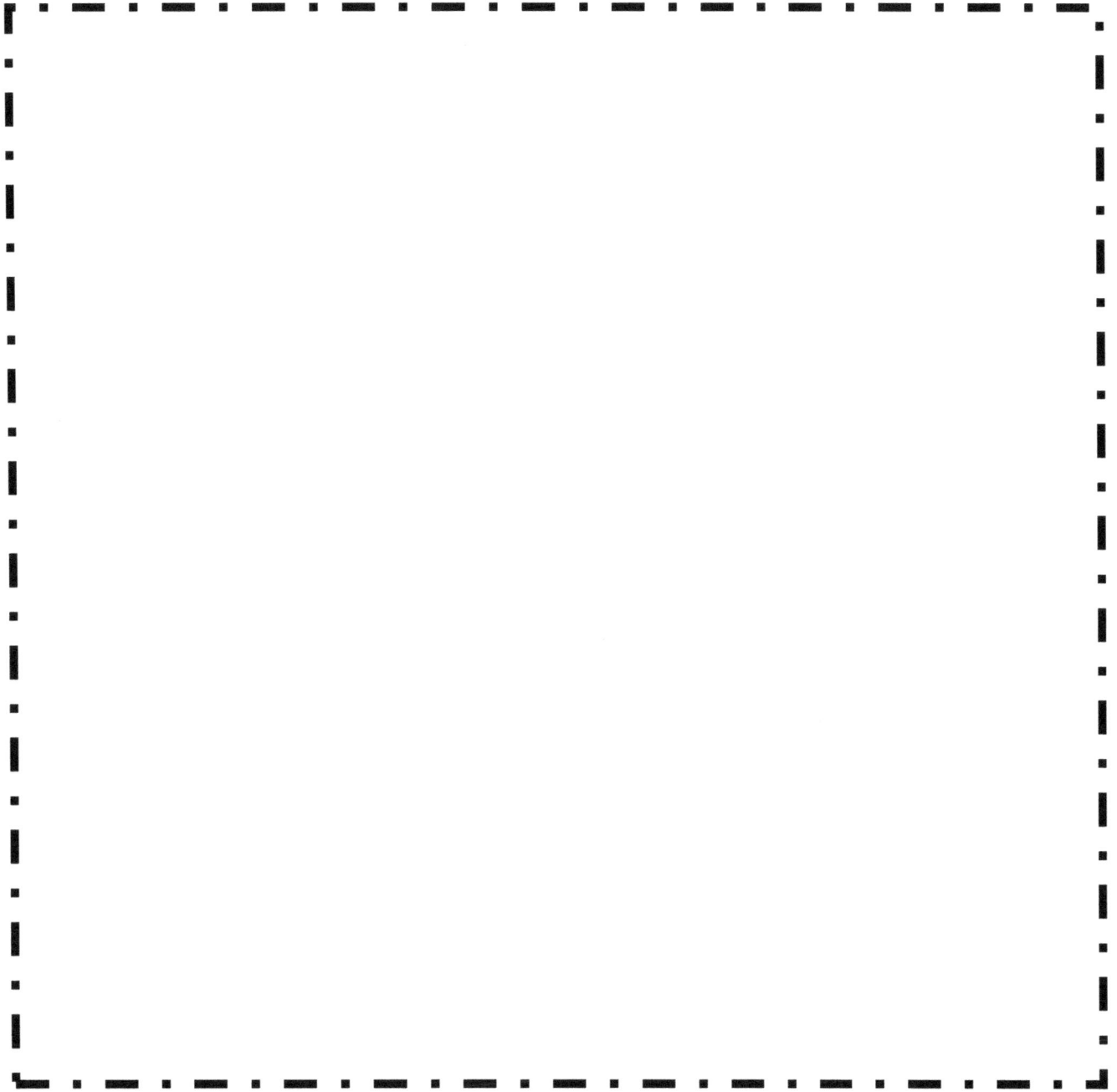

_____

_____

_____

_____

_____

40DaysOfGreater.com
Prayer Journals & Coloring Prayer Companions